| Centre number |
| Candidate number |
| Surname and initials |

 **Examining Group**

General Certificate of Secondary Education

Biology
Higher Tier
Exam 2 Paper 2

Time: one and a half hours

Instructions to candidates

Write your name, centre number and candidate number in the boxes at the top of this page.

Answer ALL questions in the spaces provided on the question paper.

Show all stages in any calculations and state the units.
You may use a calculator.

Include diagrams in your answers where this may be helpful.

Information for candidates

The number of marks available is given in brackets **[2]** at the end of each question or part question.

The marks allocated and the spaces provided for your answers are a good indication of the length of answer required.

 Where you see this icon you will be awarded marks for the quality of written communication in your answers.
This means, for example, that you should:
- write in sentences
- use correct spelling, punctuation and grammar
- use correct scientific terms.

For Examiner's use only
1
2
3
4
5
6
7
8
9
10
11
Total

© 2003 Letts Educational

1 Below is a food chain from the River Murk, which was surveyed in 1960. The data shown is the amount of a pesticide, DDT, which is now banned. Units are given in parts per million.

	Phyto-plankton →	Zoo-plankton →	Small fish →	Large fish →	Heron
Pesticide ppm	0.2	2.0	20.0	60.0	180.0

(a) Name the following:

(i) Primary consumer ....

(ii) Producer ....

(iii) Tertiary consumer .... **[3]**

(b) How many times greater is the DDT in the small fish compared to phytoplankton?

Show your working.

.... **[2]**

(c) Suggest how the pesticide was able to enter the water.

....

.... **[1]**

(d) Explain the **change** in concentration of DDT along the food chain.

....

....

....

.... **[3]**

(Total 9 marks)

© Letts Educational 2003

2 The diagram shows a blood clot.

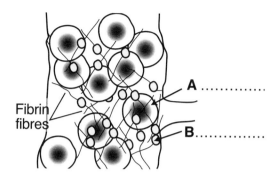

(a) Label parts A and B on the lines provided. [2]

(b) What are the functions of:

  (i) fibrin fibres?

  ....

  .... [1]

  (ii) blood clots?

  ....

  ....

  .... [2]

(c) The flow diagram shows the process of blood clotting which results from a cut in the skin.

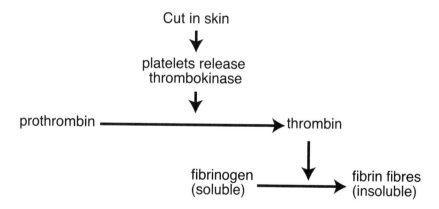

Use the flow diagram and your own knowledge to answer the following questions.

(i) What must be damaged in the skin to stimulate the production of thrombokinase?

.... [1]

(ii) What causes the change of prothrombin to thrombin.

.... [1]

(iii) Explain the effect that thrombin has on fibrinogen?

....

....

.... [2]

(Total 9 marks)

3 Complete the table below by writing in the number of chromosomes found in each cell.
Choose the number from the list below.
The first one has been done for you.

0   23   46

Cell	Number of chromosomes
muscle	46
sperm	
egg	
liver	
fertilised egg	
red blood cell	

[5]

(Total 5 marks)

4 Billy investigated the effect of different pH values on two enzymes, enzyme A and carbohydrase. The enzymes and substrates were kept at 37°C for one hour. The results are shown in the graph below.

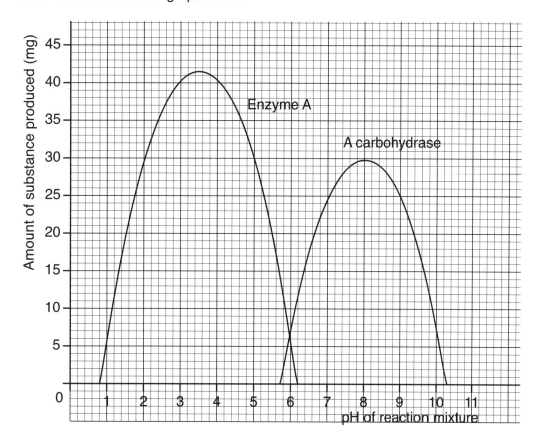

(a) (i) How much substance was produced by the carbohydrase controlled reaction at pH 7?

.... [1]

(ii) Suggest which substance was produced as the carbohydrase acted on a carbohydrate.

.... [1]

(iii) At which pH values were 30 mg of substance produced by:

1 Enzyme A

....

2 Carbohydrase.

.... [3]

(iv) One of the reactions shown takes place in the human stomach.

Which enzyme, enzyme A or carbohydrase, controls a reaction in the human stomach?

Give a reason for your answer.

.... [1]

Suggest the name of this enzyme.

.... [1]

(b) Mixtures of enzymes are used in biological washing powders.

(i) Which enzyme could be used to get rid of fat stains.

.... [1]

(ii) Explain the effect a **very high temperature** would have when using biological washing powder to wash clothes?

....

.... [2]

(Total 10 marks)

5 (a) The table below includes parts of the nitrogen cycle.

Write in the correct type of bacteria for each part of the nitrogen cycle.

Choose from the bacteria in the list below.

Nitrogen fixing bacteria

Nitrifying bacteria

Denitrifying bacteria

Part of the nitrogen cycle	Type of bacteria
Bacteria are contained in root nodules of plants in the pea and bean family	
Nitrates are changed into nitrogen gas	
Ammonia is changed into nitrites then nitrates	
Nitrogen gas is changed into nitrogen compounds	

[4]

(b) Decomposers are micro-organisms which break down organic material.

Explain the effect on decay, of cutting material up with a garden shredder before adding it to the compost heap.

....

....

.... (2)

(c) Compost heaps are turned occasionally to add air. What does the importance of supplying air indicate about the respiration of the bacteria?

.... [1]

(Total 7 marks)

© Letts Educational 2003

[turn over

6 (a) Complete the equation below to show the process of photosynthesis.

.... + ... → oxygen + ... [3]

(b) The apparatus shown below was used to measure the rate of photosynthesis.

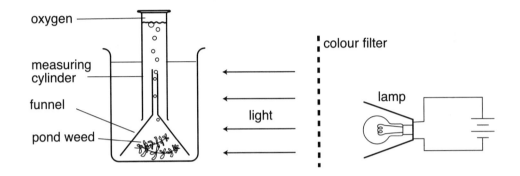

(i) Name one other piece of apparatus which would be needed to measure the **rate** of photosynthesis.

.... [1]

(ii) Given all the apparatus shown above, how would you **make sure** the pondweed was illuminated with one colour only.

....

.... [1]

(c) The bar chart below shows the volume of oxygen produced in 4 hours at 20°C by the same pondweed.

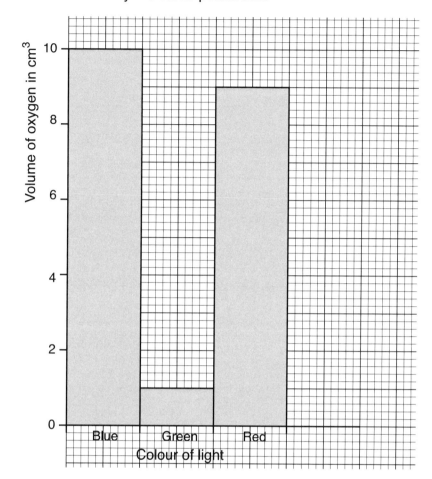

(i) Explain the results shown in the bar chart.

....

....

....

....

.... [2]

(ii) The experiment was repeated under identical conditions but white light was used to illuminate the pondweed. Explain the effect this would have.

....

.... [2]

(iii) The experiment was repeated with the same coloured lights, red, green and blue.

Explain the effect of:

increasing the temperature to 30°C,

....

....

.... [2]

decreasing the temperature to 10°C.

....

....

.... [2]

(Total 13 marks)

7   (a) The diagram below shows a synapse.

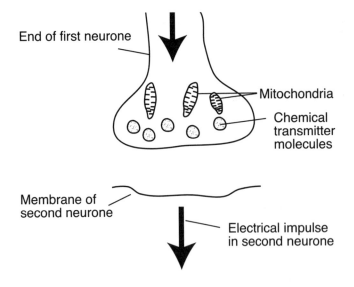

Use the information in the diagram and your own knowledge to answer the following question.

Explain the events that take place at the synapse which result in an electrical impulse being produced in the second neurone.

In this question you will be assessed on the quality of written information.

Leave blank

....

....

....

....

....

....

....

....

.... [4+1]

(b) Some drugs affect the nervous system at the synapses. Complete the sentences below by writing one or more words in each gap.

(i) Sedatives .... the speed at which an impulse from one neurone results in an impulse in the next neurone at a synapse.

An example of a sedative is alcohol.

(ii) Stimulants increase the speed at which a nerve impulse from one neurone results in an impulse in the next neurone after a synapse.

An example of a stimulant is ....

(iii) When a painkiller is used a nerve impulse from one neurone .... result in an impulse in the next neurone.

An example of a painkiller is ....

[4]

(Total 9 marks)

© Letts Educational 2003

11

[turn over

8 Diagram A shows a plant at the start of an experiment when it was illuminated from one side only. Diagram B shows the plant 3 days later, but it is not complete.

Diagram A   **Diagram B**

(a) Complete diagram B to show what the plant would look like 3 days after being illuminated from one side only. [2]

(b) The plant responds to the light coming from one side only.

 (i) Name the process which enables the plant to respond.

 .... [1]

 (ii) Name the hormone which enables the plant to respond to light from one side.

 .... [1]

 (iii) On diagram A, put a cross at a position along line X—Y to show where there would be **most** of the hormone responsible for the plant's response. [1]

 (iv) What is the advantage to the plant of the response?

 ....

 .... [2]

(Total 7 marks)

9 The diagram below shows the process of protein synthesis in a cell.

Leave blank

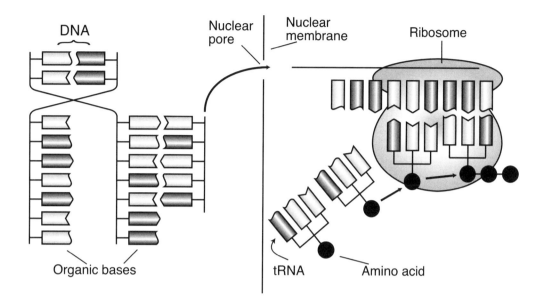

Use the information in the flow diagram and your own knowledge to answer the following question.

In this question you will be assessed on the quality of written information.

Explain the process of protein synthesis.

....

....

....

....

....

....

....

....

....

.... [5+1]

(Total 6 marks)

10 A woman's menstrual cycle lasts 28 days. The graph and diagrams below shows changes in a woman's hormone levels and some effects which took place over 36 days.

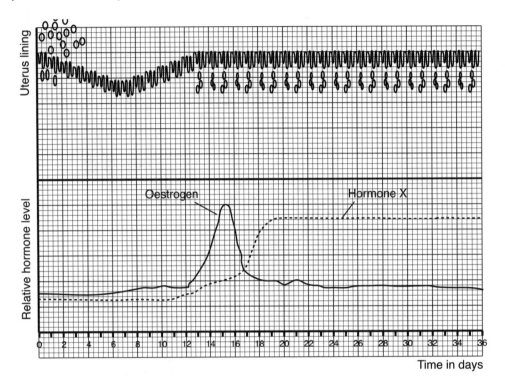

(a) Use the information in the graph and your own knowledge to answer the following questions.

(i) Suggest **two** effects which result from an increase in oestrogen.

....

.... [2]

(ii) Name hormone X.

.... [1]

(iii) On day 1 hormone X was at a low level.
What effect did this have?

.... [1]

From day 29, hormone X remained at a high level.

(iv) What effect did the high level of hormone X have?

.... [1]

(v) What important information could a doctor give to the woman as a result of the continued high level of hormone X?

....

.... [1]

(b) (i) Some women cannot produce the hormone oestrogen. Suggest an effect the lack of oestrogen would have.

.... [1]

(ii) Women can be given oestrogen tablets. Explain why it is important to give the correct dosage of oestrogen.

....

.... [2]

(Total 9 marks)

11 The diagram below shows a motor neurone linked to an organ.

not drawn to scale   A ....

Direction of impulse

B ....

(a) (i) On the diagram draw an arrow to show the direction that a nerve impulse could travel. [1]

(ii) Label parts A and B on the lines provided. [2]

(b) When you touch a very hot object you can drop it very quickly to avoid damage to your tissues. The speed of reaction is achieved by a reflex arc.

The list below includes all parts involved in a reflex arc.

| **effector** | **motor neurone** | **receptor** | **relay neurone** |
| **response** | **sensory neurone** | **stimulus** | |

Arrange them to show their correct order in a reflex arc. Some have been done for you.

stimulus → .... → .... → relay neurone →

.... → .... → response   [3]

(Total 6 marks)

BLANK PAGE

| Centre number |
| Candidate number |
| Surname and initials |

 **Examining Group**

General Certificate of Secondary Education

Biology
Higher Tier
Exam 2 Paper 1

Time: one and a half hours

Instructions to candidates

Write your name, centre number and candidate number in the boxes at the top of this page.

Answer ALL questions in the spaces provided on the question paper.

Show all stages in any calculations and state the units.
You may use a calculator.

Include diagrams in your answers where this may be helpful.

Information for candidates

The number of marks available is given in brackets **[2]** at the end of each question or part question.

The marks allocated and the spaces provided for your answers are a good indication of the length of answer required.

 Where you see this icon you will be awarded marks for the quality of written communication in your answers.
This means, for example, that you should:
- write in sentences
- use correct spelling, punctuation and grammar
- use correct scientific terms.

For Examiner's use only
1
2
3
4
5
6
7
8
9
10
Total

© 2003 Letts Educational

Answers: GCSE Biology exam 1 paper 1

Question	Answer	Mark
1 a i	membrane; cytoplasm; nucleus	3
ii	*Two from:* chloroplasts; vacuole; cell wall	2
iii	photosynthesis	1
b	*Three from:* by diffusion; through membranes; down the concentration gradient; *or* by active transport; against a concentration gradient	3

Examiner's tip
The question does not specify whether the cells concerned are those of a plant or an animal so a general answer, or one based on either, would be acceptable. With three marks available it should be obvious that simply stating 'diffusion' is not going to be enough. It is important to explain how the process takes place and not simply to describe it. You should refer to the membranes and the way concentration gradients and active transport affect the process of diffusion.

2 a i	proteins; water	2
ii	carbon; hydrogen; oxygen	2
	all three correct 2, two correct 1, 0 for other answers	
b	*first mark for appropriate vitamin/mineral salt second mark for correct function* e.g. vitamin C; maintains membranes/prevents scurvy	2
	e.g. calcium; bones/teeth	2
c	Dietary fibre adds bulk to the diet; provides something for gut muscles to work on/improves peristalsis; it retains water in the gut; it reduces chance of bowel disease/ constipation/bowel cancer.	4

Examiner's tip
An answer must address all aspects of a question or question section in order to gain full marks. Here, for example, detailed information about peristalsis alone, although commendable, would not be enough. In this section of the question you would have to refer correctly to health benefits in order to gain four marks.

3 a	*Two from:* produces carbon dioxide/wastes uses fuel uses oxygen	2
b	mitochondrion/mitochondria	1

Question	Answer	Mark
c i	removes/absorbs carbon dioxide	1
ii	control	1
iii	It would go up at Y/down at X.	1
iv	Carbon dioxide released is absorbed by KOH; oxygen is absorbed during respiration; therefore the volume/pressure in B decreases.	3

Examiner's tip
It is not sufficient simply to describe the process. Here statements about the processes involved should be followed be link-words. such as 'because', 'since' 'owing to' and 'therefore'.

4

Examiner's tip
There is a lot of information in the stem of this question. It is important that you scan it quickly the first time to get the general picture. Then read it again, very carefully, before you read the questions. You are then less likely to make careless errors.

a i	respiration	1
ii	photosynthesis	1
b	In A: colour change indicates less carbon dioxide; because the disc is photosynthesising.	2
	In B: colour change indicates more carbon dioxide; respiration is producing carbon dioxide, but there is no photosynthesis because the disc has no chlorophyll.	2
	+ 1 mark if your answer was in a logical order	1
c	No colour change indicates no change in carbon dioxide level; the muslin reduces light admitted to the disc so that photosynthesis and respiration are in balance.	3
d	In C: yellow – although the disc is green, it is not exposed to light and so photosynthesis cannot take place, only respiration. In D: yellow – the disc has only respired.	4

Examiner's tip
It is not sufficient simply to describe the processes in (b), (c) and (d). Statements about the processes involved should be followed by link-words, such as 'because', 'since', 'owing to' and 'therefore'.

© Letts Educational 2003

Question	Answer	Mark
5 a	air movement; light; temperature	3
b	It increases rate of transpiration. Water diffuses from stomatal pore down a diffusion gradient. Decreasing atmospheric humidity will increase the steepness of the gradient and therefore the rate of transpiration will also increase.	4
c	Cells lose water and therefore turgor. Since turgor provides physical support, the plant wilts.	3
6 a i	synapse	1
ii	*Three from:* neurotransmitter released at end of nerve cell; it diffuses across gap; it stimulates sensory dendrites of next cell; the impulse is initiated.	3

Examiner's tip
You are only given three lines to complete your description. The question does not demand great detail. Two or three carefully considered sentences could be enough to convey three relevant points.

b i	respiration	1
ii	after a meal	1
iii	villi/ileum/small intestine	1
iv	The rise in concentration is sensed by the pancreas; more insulin is secreted; liver cells convert glucose to glycogen; the blood glucose concentration falls.	4

Examiner's tip
Take guidance from the number of marks available and the space provided to give yourself an idea of how much detail is required. Four marks are available, therefore you should try to think of four significant things to write.

7 a	A producer is a green plant/photosynthetic plant. A herbivore is an animal that feeds exclusively on plants. A carnivore is an animal that feeds exclusively on animals.	3

Examiner's tip
The space available for your answers means that the examiner expects each of these terms to be defined very concisely. Therefore it is important that you think carefully before you launch into what might turn into a lengthy account.

Question	Answer	Mark
b	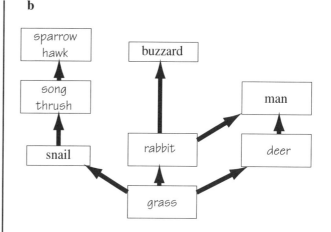	5

Examiner's tip
There is a lot of information in the table to comprehend before you start to complete the flow diagram. Read through it carefully. The answers have to interconnect correctly for the scheme to work. If you are not totally confident of your answers use a pencil for the first attempt.

c	*Five from:* respiration uses up food so mass goes down excretion of wastes, e.g. urea loss of faeces parts of plants fall off bones/feathers not retained by birds of prey/pellets coughed-up any other example, e.g. shell of snail not eaten by song thrush	5
	+ 1 mark for correct spelling, punctuation and grammar	1

Examiner's tip
It is not sufficient simply to provide a description. Here statements about the processes involved should be followed by link-words such as 'because', 'since', 'owing to' and 'therefore'. The question asks you to use examples taken from the food web to support your explanation. Make sure you do because you can assume one of the marks available will be awarded for doing so.

8 a i	deoxyribonucleic acid	1
ii	chromosomes	1
iii	*Two from:* codes for proteins some proteins function as enzymes chemistry controlled by enzymes determines outcome/features	2

© Letts Educational 2003

2 Some parts of human blood are listed below:

red blood cells   **A**
phagocytes   **B**
lymphocytes   **C**
platelets   **D**
plasma   **E**

The table below gives some of the functions of the blood.

Complete the table by writing **one** letter in each box to link each function to the correct part of the blood. You may use each letter once, more than once or not at all.

Function	Part of blood
transport of urea	E
production of antibodies	
transport of antibodies	
killing microorganisms by surrounding them then digesting them	
transport of oxygen	
transport of hormones	
helps the blood to clot	

[6]

(Total 6 marks)

3 The leaf shown was partially covered with the strip of aluminium foil and the plant was left in bright light for three days.

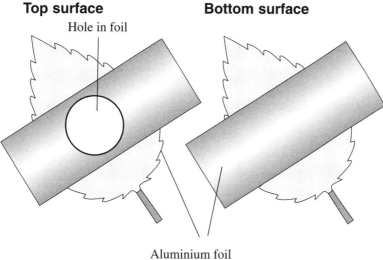

(a) After three days the leaf was removed from the plant and the starch test was carried out.

(i) On the diagram below shade in the areas which would contain starch.

Top surface

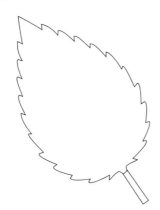

[2]

(ii) Complete the stages below by writing a word in each gap, to describe how the leaf was tested for starch.

- The leaf was dipped into boiling water to soften it.

- It was then put into boiling ………………………. in a water bath for 10 minutes to remove the green colour from the leaf.

- The leaf was then dipped into water.

Question	Answer	Mark
c	more muscle affected by oxygen and glucose starvation	1
d	getting a satisfactory heart for the patient; stay in hospital for patient; serious, invasive surgery; post-operative treatment to prevent rejection.	4
	+ 1 mark for correct scientific language	1

Examiner's tip
Take guidance from the number of marks available and the space provided to give yourself an idea of how much detail is required. There are four marks available, therefore you should try to think of four significant things to write.

Question	Answer	Mark
1 a i	A = cornea B = lens C = retina	3
ii	cornea/A; lens/B	2

Examiner's tip
These two parts bend or refract the light to enable the eye to focus. Many pupils forget the cornea bends the light as well as the lens!

| b | | becomes long and thin; become tight; contract | 3 |

Examiner's tip
Remember that in focusing a near object the opposite thing happens to each part.

c		The retina contains light sensitive cells; which are cones; These react to the red light and send; electrical impulses; along the optic nerve; to the brain. *any 5 of points shown*	5
		+ 1 mark for correct spelling, punctuation and grammar	1
2		C; E; B; A; E; E or D	6

Examiner's tip
Examiners often give you a starting point which you can build on logically. Note that both plasma and platelets have major roles in clotting of blood.

| 3 a i |  | 2 |

Examiner's tip
Note that the parts exposed to light need to be shaded. A and B candidates even remember to shade the shape in the middle of the foil!

ii	• The leaf was dipped into boiling water to soften it. • It was then put into boiling **ethanol**; in a water bath for 10 minutes to remove the green colour from the leaf. • The leaf was then dipped into water. • It was laid flat in a Petri dish and **iodine**; solution was poured over the leaf. The parts which contained starch turned a **blue/black**; colour.	3
c	no light received; so no photosynthesis	2
d	Respiration	1

Examiner's tip
Always remember that energy can be released from starch in respiration!

© Letts Educational 2003   6

Question	Answer	Mark
4 a		

food substance	enzyme	breaks down into
starch	amylase	maltose (sugar)
protein	*protease* or *pepsin*	amino acids
fats and oils	lipase	*fatty acid* and *glycerol*

4

Examiner's tip
Incomplete tables like this give you clues. This table includes the important enzyme controlled reactions for most GCSE Exam Boards. Learn them!

b A No product is made/enzyme inactive;
no collisions between substrate molecules and active sites of enzymes. 2

B Maximum amount of product made;
many successful collisions between substrate molecules and active sites of enzymes. 2

C No product made;
Enzyme is destroyed/ enzyme denatured/ active site destroyed permanently. 2

Examiner's tip
Never state that enzymes are killed: not true and no mark!

5 a   Route   Part
1   lungs
2   **pulmonary vein**
3   left atrium
4   **left ventricle**
5   **aorta**
6   **renal artery**
7   kidney
8   **renal vein**
9   **vena cava**
10   **right atrium** or **right ventricle**
11   **pulmonary artery**
12   lungs   5
take 1mark off for each incorrect pair

Examiner's tip
Take care with arteries and veins. An artery takes blood from the heart to an organ. A vein takes blood from an organ towards the heart.

b   Prevents the backflow of blood/ makes sure the blood goes in one direction only. 1

6 a i   *Either*
Blood glucose falls;

Question	Answer	Mark

sensory neurones detect level;
so pancreas secretes glucagon into blood;
liver responds by changing glycogen into glucose;
glucose leaves liver;
blood glucose rises again so less glucagon produced.
or
Blood glucose rises;
sensory neurones detect level;
so pancreas secretes insulin into blood;
glucose enters liver;
liver responds by changing glucose into glycogen;
blood glucose falls again so less insulin produced. 4

Examiner's tip
Always explain negative feedback in this way: the more of a hormone that is produced, the more it leads to its own decrease.
Either of the two ways of giving the answer above are acceptable.

ii   pancreas secretes insulin;
results in glucose entering the liver/and cells;
so blood glucose level decreases. 3

b i   diabetes 1

ii   1 control diet by low carbohydrate intake;
2 inject into blood stream; insulin. 3

Examiner's tip
Note that insulin must be injected into the bloodstream. Insulin is a protein and we would digest it if it was in tablet form.

7 a   along a chromosome 1
b   An allele is a different form of a gene 1
c i   3 1
ii   2 1
iii   Sufferer/has Huntingdon's chorea 1
d i

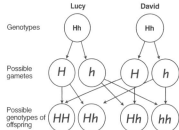

2

5 The diagram below shows the blood circulation in the human body.

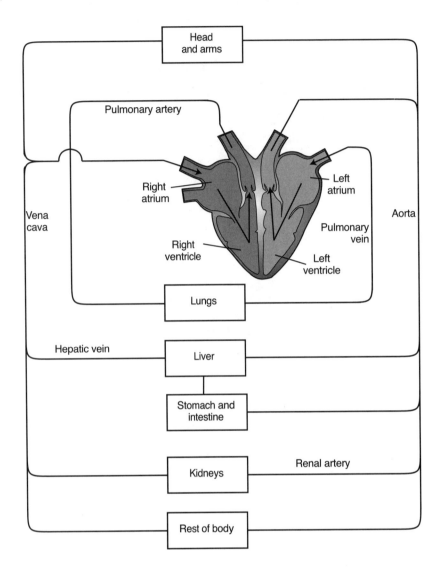

(a) List the parts in the correct order to show the shortest route taken by an oxygen molecule as it passes from the lungs to the kidneys, then returns to the lungs as part of a carbon dioxide molecule. Refer only to the parts which have been labelled on the diagram.

Leave blank

Write your list in the table below. Some parts have been completed for you.

Route	Part
1	lungs
2	
3	left atrium
4	
5	
6	
7	kidneys
8	
9	
10	
11	
12	lungs

[5]

(b) What is the function of a valve in the heart?

....

.... [1]

(Total 6 marks)

© Letts Educational 2003   9   **[turn over**

Question	Answer	Mark

Examiner's tip
Take care to remember the role of each type of bacteria. Do not mix them up!

b greater rate of decay,
because surface area increased,
so bacteria are in contact with more surface
material to decay   **2**
any two points

c Aerobic respiration   **1**

Examiner's tip
The key information is that oxygen is needed in aerobic respiration.

6 a Water + carbon dioxide → glucose + oxygen   **3**

Examiner's tip
Photosynthesis is included in around 100% of biology papers. It's so important to revise this topic!

b i stopwatch/ stopclock   **1**

ii Put apparatus in a dark room apart **and** use the filter/
Cover apparatus with a box to exclude extra light and use the filter.   **1**

Examiner's tip
Always draw on your experience of investigation work in school. Transfer your ideas to different investigations in exam papers.

c i Different coloured lights allow the pondweed to photosynthesise at different rates;
Blue is the best light for photosynthesis from the three tested;
Green is the worst light for photosynthesis from the three tested.   **2**
Any two for maximum marks

Examiner's tip
Often a mark scheme will show more points than can actually be awarded marks. Examiners give marks up to a maximum. Here that maximum is 2.

ii With white light the amount of photosynthesis would be greater;
white light contains a mixture and includes all of the other colours so it will be greater.   **2**

Question	Answer	Mark

iii Rate of photosynthesis would increase/more oxygen produced;
nearer to optimum temperature/better conditions for the enzymes/more collisions of enzyme with substrate.   **2**
Rate of photosynthesis would decrease/less oxygen produced;
further from optimum temperature/conditions not as suitable for the enzymes/
fewer collisions of enzyme with substrate.   **2**

Examiner's tip
Always be ready to interpret data given in a question. Look for the relationships shown by the data.

7 a (electrical) impulse from first neurone;
causes transmitter molecules to be secreted into the synapse or gap/
causes acetylcholine or noradrenaline molecules to be secreted into the synapse;
mitochondria help release energy/ process needs energy;
transmitter molecules pass into
second neurone;   **4**
this finally results in the electrical impulse in second neurone. (No mark as given in question.)

Examiner's tip
Here is a situation where you need to interpret given information and use your own knowledge. An electrical impulse is needed to start the process. Never state that an impulse actually crosses a synapse. It does not! What actually happens is that chemical transmitter substances pass across the synaptic gap which may then result in an impulse in the next nerve cell.

Communication mark
One mark awarded for using a suitable structure and style in writing.   **1**

Examiner's tip
Give your answer logically with good grammar to score this mark.

i slow down
ii amphetamine/speed/caffeine/cocaine
iii cannot; aspirin/paracetamol/
ibuprofen/heroin/morphine   **4**

© Letts Educational 2003

Question	Answer	Mark
8 a	plant shoot has grown higher; the shoot bends towards light	2

Examiner's tip
Note, the bend must begin after the original height of plant in diagram A.

b	i	phototropism	1
	ii	auxin	1
	iii	Cross drawn nearer the X than the Y; (X---x--------Y)	1

Examiner's tip
The auxin is found on the left side. It causes a greater amount of cell division on that side so it grows more strongly, and pushes towards the right side. Remember this for your GCSE exam.

	iv	Get more light; So more photosynthesis.	2

Examiner's tip
More light, more photosynthesis and therefore (perhaps) the plant is a better competitor than other plants.

9	First stage takes place in the nucleus; DNA unwinds to expose bases; mRNA forms along the DNA strand/ DNA codes for mRNA; mRNA moves through nuclear membrane; tRNA links to the mRNA; each tRNA molecule carries an amino acid; each sequence of three bases code for a specific amino acid (*given either for tRNA or mRNA*); a sequence of amino acids link together; a polypeptide is formed.	5

any 5 points given

Examiner's tip
Note that in this type of longer response question you are given a lot of diagramatic information. This is supplied to stimulate your memory and give you a structure for your answer. Follow the information logically to score the marks.

	Communication mark: One mark awarded for ensuring that a suitable structure and style of writing is given.	1

Examiner's tip
Basically if you are logical in your explanation you will score the mark. Give your information clearly!

Question	Answer	Mark
10 a	i	build up of the lining of uterus/ build up of endometrium; stimulates increase in hormone X; stimulates ovulation/ stimulates luteinising hormone	2

any 2 points for 2 marks

	ii	progesterone	1
	iii	resulted in menstruation	1
	iv	maintained the lining of the uterus/ kept the lining or endometrium in place	1
	v	woman was pregnant	1

Examiner's tip
Note that with graphs and associated events shown along the timescale, an event is likely to correspond to peaks and troughs.

b	i	women would not ovulate/ lining of uterus would not build / lining of uterus would not repair	1

Examiner's tip
Oestrogen is responsible for many female characteristics such as breast development. This is not credited here due to the central theme of the question, menstrual cycle, stressed at the beginning of the question.

	ii	if dosage too small then still no ovulation; if dosage too big then there are multiple births/ too many ova released.	2
11 a	i	horizontal arrow to the right	1

Examiner's tip
Remember that in a sensory neurone the impulse moves in the opposite direction.

	ii	A = muscle B = axon	2

Examiner's tip
Did you know the parts? In your exam it may be the other parts of the neurone which need to be labelled.

b	stimulus → **receptor** → **sensory neurone** → relay neurone → **motor neurone** → **effector** → response	4

Examiner's tip
Asked to give the complete reflex arc you may struggle, but here the examiner gives you a structure which stimulates your memory. You get a lot of help but without your own revision the question would be impossible.

© Letts Educational 2003

(ii) How many people included in the genetic diagram are homozygous?

.... [1]

(iii) What is the phenotype of Mr Simms?

.... [1]

(d) Complete the genetic diagram below to show the possible genotypes if Lucy and David have children.

(i)

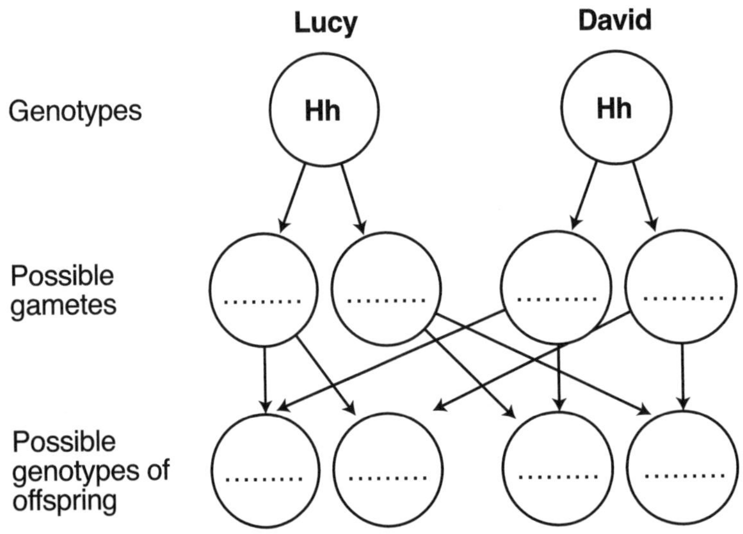

Lucy — Hh   David — Hh

Genotypes

Possible gametes: ....

Possible genotypes of offspring: ....

[2]

(ii) What is the chance of producing a child who suffers from Huntingdon's chorea?

.... [1]

(iii) What is the chance of producing a baby girl who does not suffer from Huntingdon's chorea?

.... [1]

(e) The symptoms of Huntingdon's chorea do not appear until a person is about 30–40 years of age.

Explain the effect this may have on the rate at which the disease is spread through the population?

....

....

.... [2]

(Total 11 marks)

8 (a) Complete the following passage by filling in the gaps to show how acid rain is formed.

The pollutant which causes acid rain is released into the air when

.... are burned. .... is given off into the air.

An example when this gas is produced is at coal burning power stations and

from .... The gas mixes with water vapour in the clouds and

.... is formed. [4]

(b) Explain effects of acid rain on:

(i) plants

....

(ii) herbivores

....

.... [3]

(Total 7 marks)

WHAT IS NEEDED FOR A GRADE A?

Contrary to many people's beliefs, grade A is not determined each year by awarding the grade to a fixed percentage of candidates or by awarding a grade A to those candidates who achieve a fixed mark. It is done by inspection of the papers and awarding grade A to those candidates who meet the criteria that have been agreed nationally for grade A.

A grade A candidate should be able to:

1. use detailed knowledge and understanding to devise a strategy for a task;
2. identify key factors in the task and control conditions;
3. make predictions;
4. present data appropriately and use knowledge from different sources;
5. recognise and explain anomalous results;
6. draw appropriate graphs choosing suitable axes;
7. use scientific knowledge and understanding to draw conclusions;
8. identify shortcomings in evidence;
9. use a range of apparatus with the correct precision and skill:
10. make precise measurements and systematic observations;
11. select which observations and measurements are relevant;
12. recall information from all areas of the specification;
13. use detailed scientific knowledge and understanding in a range of applications;
14. detect patterns and draw conclusions when information comes from different sources;
15. draw information together and communicate knowledge effectively;
16. use scientific or mathematical conventions to support arguments;
17. use a wide range of scientific and technical vocabulary.

Some of these criteria can be met in Coursework (Sc1) but most can also be demonstrated in written papers.

WHAT EXTRA IS REQUIRED FOR AN A* GRADE?

Having established what is required to be awarded a Grade A you might be interested to know what is required for an A* grade. There are at present no A* criteria.

When the Awarding committee is awarding grades it is asked to fix marks for Grade A and Grade C. This is done paper by paper. Suppose on a particular paper the Grade A mark was fixed at 70 and the grade C mark at 50. (These numbers have been chosen only to keep the arithmetic that follows simple). The Grade B mark is then fixed arithmetically half way between 50 and 70, i.e. 60. The Grade A* is then fixed the same number of marks above A as B is below it. In the example we have used A* would be fixed at 80. At this point it would be customary to look at papers around this mark to confirm that they were worthy of A*. What does this tell you? Grade A* is a very high standard and relatively few are awarded.

As there are no criteria it is not as clear what examiners are looking for as it is at Grade A. The following points may help you.

- Generally as the Grade A* boundary is a high mark, there is no scope for a bad answer to any question on the paper. A grade A* candidate scores well on questions.
- A grade A* candidate uses scientific language routinely and confidently. It is worthwhile working through a glossary of scientific terms or a scientific dictionary to clarify the exact meaning of all terms and then trying to use them correctly.
- A grade A* candidate brings information from different parts of the specification together in an answer.
- Grade A* candidates in Biology have a clear idea of the kinetic model for particles in solids, liquids and gases and the lock and key model in enzymes. They can use these ideas of models to explain ideas such as osmosis, diffusion, transpiration and rates of enzyme reactions.
- Grade A* candidates in Biology also have a good understanding of ideas such as genetic engineering, genetics and DNA replications. They should also have an opinion and be able to present scientifically reasoned arguments on social issues such as genetically modified foods or the use of transgenic organisms as organ donors.
- Also Grade A* candidates score highly in calculations. They also give answers to the correct number of significant figures and with correct units.

(b) After stage 5, the genetically engineered bacteria are put into an industrial fermenter.

(i) A suitable temperature is needed to enable the bacteria to reproduce effectively.

Explain how this condition can be achieved.

....

.... [2]

(ii) Why do the bacteria need a suitable temperature to reproduce effectively?

....

.... [1]

(Total 9 marks)

| Centre number |
| Candidate number |
| Surname and initials |

Examining Group

General Certificate of Secondary Education

Biology
Higher Tier
Exam 1   Paper 2

Time: one hour

For Examiner's use only	
1	
2	
3	
4	
5	
6	
Total	

Instructions to candidates

Write your name, centre number and candidate number in the boxes at the top of this page.

Answer ALL questions in the spaces provided on the question paper.

Show all stages in any calculations and state the units.
You may use a calculator.

Include diagrams in your answers where this may be helpful.

Information for candidates

The number of marks available is given in brackets **[2]** at the end of each question or part question.

The marks allocated and the spaces provided for your answers are a good indication of the length of answer required.

 Where you see this icon you will be awarded marks for the quality of written communication in your answers.
This means, for example, that you should:
- write in sentences
- use correct spelling, punctuation and grammar
- use correct scientific terms.

© 2003 Letts Educational

1 (a) The diagram shows a generalised fermenter.

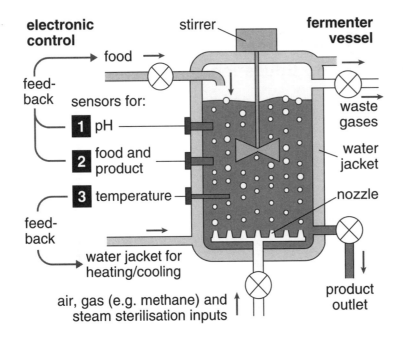

(i) Give **two** environmental factors that are controlled in the fermenter shown.

....

.... [2]

(ii) Why would a user want to introduce steam into the fermenter?

....

.... [1]

(b) What is meant by **(1) batch culture** and **(2) immobilised enzymes** in the context of fermenter technology?

1 ....

....

....

2 ....

....

.... **[4]**

(c) Give **two** advantages to manufacturers of employing continuous culture rather than batch culture.

1 ....

....

2 ....

.... **[2]**

(Total 9 marks)

© Letts Educational 2003   3   **[turn over**

2 Use the information in the following text and your general knowledge of biology to answer questions (a) to (g).

> The bacterium *Agrobacterium* has circular pieces of DNA called plasmids. One type of plasmid contains genetic information that accelerates cell division inducing tumour formation. They are called Ti-plasmids. Genes controlling desirable features from another organism can be inserted into these plasmids. A gene that confers resistance to antibiotics is usually introduced at the same time.
>
> When Agrobacterium infects a plant cell its DNA becomes part of one of the plant cell's chromosomes – part of its genetic make-up. *Agrobacterium* can be used in this way to genetically engineer a crop plant.
>
> Cells are taken from the crop plant to be modified. The cell walls are removed to make infection easier. This is done using cellulase enzymes under carefully controlled conditions. Cells which have had their walls removed are called protoplasts.
>
> Protoplasts are placed into a dish containing nutrient solution. A culture of *Agrobacterium*, containing modified Ti-plasmids, is added to the protoplasts. The protoplasts are removed after several days incubation. They are plated out onto nutrient agar. The agar jelly contains an antibiotic.
>
> Surviving protoplasts are harvested after a period of growth. Micropropagation techniques are then used to produce a complete plant from each cell establishing a clone with the new, desired features.

(a) In what way do plasmids differ from normal chromosomes?

....

.... [1]

(b) What are Ti-plasmids?

....

.... [1]

(c) What is meant by the term **transgenic**?

....

.... [1]

(d) Why are the crop plant cells treated with cellulase enzymes early in the process described in the paragraphs above?

....

....

....

.... **[2]**

(e) Suggest a reason for introducing a gene that confers resistance to antibiotics when the Ti-plasmid was formed.

....

....

....

.... **[3]**

(f) Explain how the protoplasts, *harvested after a period of growth*, form the basis for a clone of plants with the desired features.

....

....

....

.... **[3]**

(g) Suggest one example, with a reason, of a feature that would be a desirable modification in crop plants.

....

....

....

.... **[2]**

(Total 13 marks)

Leave blank

© Letts Educational 2003

5

[turn over

3 (a) The diagram shows the effect of pH on the rate of reaction of two enzymes.

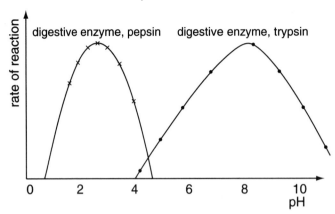

(i) An enzyme has an optimum pH, that is, the pH at which it works best. What is the optimum pH for trypsin?

.................pH 8... [1]

(ii) What is the approximate range of pH over which pepsin is active?

.... [1]

(b) Biological detergents may contain proteases and lipases.

(i) Explain the part these enzymes play in getting clothes clean.

You will be given credit for spelling, punctuation and grammar.

....

....

....

....

....

.... [6+1]

(ii) Why do biological powder manufacturers recommend that these powders should be used at lower temperatures than non-biological washing powders?

....

.... [1]

(Total 10 marks)

4 **(a)** Complete the table.
Your answer should include three diseases caused by different types of microorganisms.

infectious disease	type of organism causing the disease	means of spread

[6]

(b) **(i)** Name a genetic disease.

.... [1]

(ii) Use appropriate genetic terms to explain how this disease is inherited.
You may find it helpful to add symbols and notes to the diagram provided.

....

....

....

....

.... [4]

(Total 11 marks)

5 **(a)** Explain how the human body can recognise its own cells and can tell when there are 'foreign' cells present.

....

.... **[2]**

(b) When foreign cells get into the body, e.g. during a bacterial infection for the first time, an immune response is initiated. During this primary immune response two groups of cells are produced.

(i) What are these two groups of cells called?

1 ....

2 .... **[2]**

(ii) What are the jobs of the two groups of cells?

1 ....

....

2 ....

.... **[2]**

(Total 6 marks)

© Letts Educational 2003

6 The diagram shows a heart which has undergone bypass surgery.

(a) Label A and B. [2]

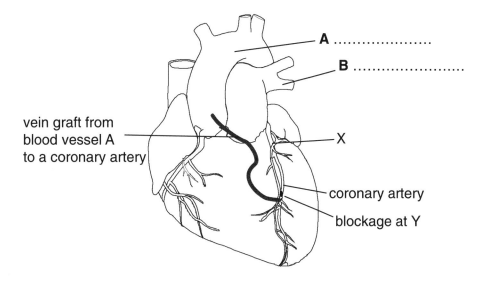

(b) Explain how blockages in coronary arteries affect the heart's ability to work.

....

....

.... [3]

(c) Suggest why a blockage occuring at X is likely to have more serious consequences than one occuring at Y.

....

.... [1]

(d) Describe the problems associated with having a whole heart transplant as a means of treating heart disease.

You will be given credit for use of correct scientific language.

....

....

....

....

.... [4+1]

(Total 11 marks)

BLANK PAGE

BLANK PAGE

BLANK PAGE